YOUR KNOWLEDGE HAS VALUE

- We will publish your bachelor's and master's thesis, essays and papers

- Your own eBook and book - sold worldwide in all relevant shops

- Earn money with each sale

Upload your text at www.GRIN.com and publish for free

Bahanur Alişoğlu

Turkey and EU - What Does the Society Think?

GRIN Verlag

Bibliografische Information der Deutschen Nationalbibliothek:

Die Deutsche Bibliothek verzeichnet diese Publikation in der Deutschen National-
bibliografie; detaillierte bibliografische Daten sind im Internet über http://dnb.d-
nb.de/ abrufbar.

Imprint:

Copyright © 2012 GRIN Verlag GmbH
Druck und Bindung: Books on Demand GmbH, Norderstedt Germany
ISBN: 978-3-656-13874-7

This book at GRIN:

http://www.grin.com/en/e-book/188879/turkey-and-eu-what-does-the-society-think

GRIN - Your knowledge has value

Der GRIN Verlag publiziert seit 1998 wissenschaftliche Arbeiten von Studenten, Hochschullehrern und anderen Akademikern als eBook und gedrucktes Buch. Die Verlagswebsite www.grin.com ist die ideale Plattform zur Veröffentlichung von Hausarbeiten, Abschlussarbeiten, wissenschaftlichen Aufsätzen, Dissertationen und Fachbüchern.

Visit us on the internet:

http://www.grin.com/

http://www.facebook.com/grincom

http://www.twitter.com/grin_com

Turkey and EU: What Does the Society Think?

Bahanur Alişoğlu

Universidade do Minho

Turkey and EU: What Does the Society Think?

Abstract

The aim of this study is to understand the fatiguing relationship between Turkey and European Union which has been lasting for four decades and to come to perceive whether Turkey is a proper candidate or not when examined carefully. There are some debates over Turkish society and its approach to European Union which reinforces Turkey to change in terms of social structures such as policy and economy. This study is also to be prepared in order to explain what has a big impact on Europe's viewpoint about Turkey and Turkishness. Moreover, some Turks' opposition to European Union is added to the study. When doing this study, it has been read several sources and articles by well-known Turkish authors and teachers as well as foreign researchers who keep an eye on Turkey and EU relations. In light of that study, Turkey and EU relations might be told in another words and be understood that some historical and cultural effects can determine what society thinks.

Keywords: Turkey and European Union, Turkish society, Turkish army, Turks' migration.

Turkey and EU: What Does the Society Think?

A Brief History of EU and Turkey

Turkey and European Union relations so far have been studied and searched by several academicians, students as well as politicians since it has a bizarre history that continues between the collocutors but does not come to an end at all. The fact that Turkey and European Union relations are tense and vague make this subject more intriguing. I would like to start to write my essay by giving some crucial details about how and when Turkey and European Union relations began before going into the deep details such as the reasons why EU does not want Turkey to participate or why Turkish citizens oppose to EU relations.

EU and Turkey started to negotiate in the early 1960's, approximately when Greece had applied for full membership. Turkey had a good image in the World's eyes since it participated in NATO and assisted the peace whole heartedly by supporting USA and accordingly USA's allies at the Korean War which occurred between 1950 and 1953. Turkey was naturally supposed to be a part of European Union as it proved itself with NATO. However, Turkey was very unlucky in terms of timing. By the time Turkey applied for a full membership, the military intervention erupted and the negotiations were postponed until September 12, 1963. Moreover, at that time EC became under Gaullist pressure which was not very good for Turkey at all. Turkey's European identity and such issues had been questioned by several EU countries, but especially by France that did not seem to intend to accept Turkey as a part of Europe. Eventually, the Ankara Association Agreement was signed between Turkey and EU so that they could start the negotiations despite of all negative and unfortunate events that undermined the EU and Turkey relations. The agreement became effective in 1964. On this agreement, there were three stages for Turkey and EU relations called preparatory, transitional and final stages. The first one called preparatory stage was a period which was intended to provide financial aid to Turkey so that it could take proper measures in order to develop its economy and prepare itself for the transitional stage. The transitional stage was a process that Turkey had to involve in a customs union between 12 and 22 years that might bring the full membership to Turkey. It never happened, though. Turkey assumed that those stages were guarantees for full membership and never wanted to be left behind Greece. Yet, Greece participated in European Union before Turkey as known. At the 70's and 80's, the case for Turkey was not brilliant. In these decades, in Turkey lots of problems emerged that could be listed as political, economical and social. Those problems which were derived from different sources did not help Turkey improve its relations with European Union. Nor could Turkey expect European Union to tolerate this issue. First of all, the Cyprus crisis, that was between Turkey and Greece for Cyprus Island's Greek and Turkish citizens, gave a big harm to EU and Turkey relations. Meanwhile, a new military junta took place at the heart of policy in Turkey. Although Turkey tried to heal this case by taking various precautions, European Union urgently deactivated the process until the 1980's.

In the 1980's, Turkish economy as well as policy had some major changes. In the economy, a new era started which can be associated with liberalization. Then Prime Minister Turgut Özal, was much more enthusiastic about European Union and had a tendency to improve democracy and the economy of Turkey in order to meet the EU's high expectations. After all the vital breakthroughs that Turkey worked on, Turkey's insistency for the full membership of EU was indispensible. European Union hesitated for a long while which lasted for 30 months and in the end, instead of full membership, Turkey was offered to complete customs union framework before having a full membership status. European Union came up with some crucial reasons about why they were unable to accept Turkey then. At that time, Berlin Wall coincided with the EU Commission's decision. The Cold War seemed to disappear slowly and Turkey was worried about its special status as a strategic partner of the West against Soviet

Union inasmuch it was an essential reason about why EU might need Turkey as a good ally. Speaking of the facts, Turkey was lingered for years by European Union by used custom union. Both sides were aware of that but none spoke out about that. European Union could neither accept Turkey nor turn its back to this country for some obvious reasons. Unstable relationship among them made Turkey think about it and it led Turkey to Central Asia. Turkey seemed to be uninterested in EU for a while and started to visit brother countries. That wise bluff of Turkey concerned Europeans because they did not want to lose their impacts on Turkey. They supposedly awarded Turkey by giving an official 'candidate' status in 1999. It rejoiced then Turkish parliament and the new negotiations started until the new power party as known as AKP (Justice and Development Party) began to rule Turkey in 2002.

European Relations During AKP Governance

AKP started to govern Turkey in 2002 and since then, they have been power there. AKP is a right-sided conservative party that mainly focuses on Islamic countries and Islamic life style as known. However, since AKP began ruling Turkey, one of their primary aims was to be a part of Europe. They claimed that Turkey would be better off with European Union in terms of economy. They made some important and permanent changes on Turkish policy and economy including the foreign affairs related to EU relations. The leader of AKP, Tayyip Erdoğan is reputation for his outspoken status about EU and some sensitive subjects such as Armenian Genocide issue that Europe frequently indicates whenever talked about human rights and historical debates over Turkey. AKP strongly believed that Turkey has to change over. According to some elites and left-sided groups, AKP aims at being an Islamic country like the Arab countries that Tayyip Erdoğan has good and deep relations with. It also concerns European Union as they seem not to be fond of a new union that might threaten the Western World. AKP still considers European Union and always says that it is of crucial importance

Turkey and EU: What Does the Society Think?

For Turkey to have full membership. Yet, PM Erdoğan implies that he ran out of patience as EU has been prolonging this process in four decades leaving Turkey in limbo all the time. Last year, in a press conference he told that there was no point in bothering with European Union. He offered to put all money on better relations with Arab countries.[1] It is a fact that Erdoğan is very popular over Arab countries as he makes a statement about Islam against Israel and EU countries. He is respected by Arab leaders as well as citizens. It may seem like a suspicious situation as AKP both wants to participate in EU which Christianity dominates and protects its Islamic roots. Yet, it is also other subject that academicians and Turkish elites have been dwelling on.

Why Does EU oppose to Turkey's Membership?

In the previous section, I have mentioned the recent years of Turkey and EU relations. In fact, EU and Turkey relations are based on the 11th century, when Turks came to minor Asia as known as Anatolia today. Since then, Turkey has been in a relationship with European countries. After Sultan Mehmet conquered İstanbul which was called Constantinople by the Byzantine and still today's Greeks, The Ottoman Empire came closer to Europe and became a gigantic danger for European Kingdoms. The Ottomans involved in many wars with European countries and also investigated European culture, social life and economy as well as policy. I am of opinion that we should also concentrate on the historical debates as they determine the EU and Turkey relations today. History cannot be separated from policy. Nor can we ignore the historical reasons about European Union and Turkey relations. Since the Ottomans were reputation for glories, Europe was very afraid to be conquered by Turks. This fear caused prejudices and sometimes hatred. Still, the counties like Austria show the Ottomans in the

---

[1] The news can be found on Hürriyet Daily News:
http://www.hurriyetdailynews.com/default.aspx?pageid=438&n=is-the-eu-still-important-for-the-akp-2010-06-15

history as one of the reasons why Turkey cannot be a European Union country. They ignore the Republic of Turkey which was found the great leader Mustafa Kemal Atatürk and prefer to remind Turks of the history as if to hold grudge. They seem to believe that Turkish people still live the Ottoman era in Turkey in terms of social life and religion. That must be taken into the consideration when mentioned EU's opposition to Turkey. Turkey came across some obstacles in the 1990's. European Union had some vital reasons not to accept Turkey's membership as I mentioned above. These obstacles can be listed by made use of Erkan Erdoğdu's work named 'Turkey and Europe: Undivided but not United' (2002).

- Major structural disparities between EC and Turkey
- High levels of inflation, unemployment and industrial protection
- Low levels of social protection
- Inadequate human rights provisions
- Turkey's problems with "one Member State of the Community" (i.e. Greece)

When considered the main rejection reasons, we can see the main problem is that Turkey's deficiency in the field of human rights, unemployment, education and economics. However, there are some hidden reasons in these points that may consist of the real reasons about Turkey's membership. The religion, Turkish Army's sharp and strong voice and fear of Turks' migration to Europe factors are not mentioned here but also not forgotten under any circumstances. It is a fact that European Union is a Christian organization that was made up of Christian countries mainly. Turkey may be a secular country in terms of its policy but the rising Islamist parties in last decades and the current power party of Turkish Republic proved that Islam was the main religion in Turkey which had been highly protected by the conservative side of Turkish policy and society. It may still remind Europeans of the Crusades that took place between Christians and Muslims for a long time in the past. When examined

7

carefully, Europe conservative Christian parties seem to be more worried by the existence of Turkey in Europe than the other parties. That Germany has already spoken out about that issue could be a good proof. The religion factor cannot be disregarded in foreign affairs since it might have a crucial impact on the given decisions. That might be one of the reasons why European Union does not avoid raising voice about Turkey's Muslim identity.

One of the main reasons why European Union is cool on Turkey's membership is that Turkey has a big army which affected the Turkish politics in the past with juntas by the time Europe started to negotiations with Turkey. Europe had a tendency to think that Turkey was a military country like Burma. Turkey's democracy was interrupted by military juntas several times and the politicians whose opinions were not the same with the army were put into the police custody. Lots of students died in fighting over the politics and some politicians experienced the executions. The Army declared that those who did not agree with democracy would have to live the same unfortunate events like the others. Turkey did not experience the dictatorship era like Portugal, Spain or Greece but Turkish policy was always under control of Turkish Army. Three years ago, a so-called plan named Ergenekon[2] erupted suddenly around the new government. AKP started to interrogations of some army members such as then generals or retired soldiers as well as the journalists who were in these events. These people were detailed by AKP government since they supposedly wanted to destroy the government and establish a military country. AKP thought that to put those who were responsible for the juntas in jail would be a brilliant idea in terms of EU and Turkey relations but it did not do the trick as assumed. EU thinks that keeping them in prison for a long time without submitting valid and clear proves is against fundamental human rights. Now, these people still are in jail and have been waiting for the day they are going to the court and learn what they have done to deserve

---

[2] For further information about Ergenekon:
http://www.todayszaman.com/newsDetail_getNewsById.action?load=detay&link=143502

that.

Speaking of the social facts that have a big impact on European countries and accordingly EU it would be wise to mention Turks' migration to Europe that started almost four decades ago. Turks began to migrate to Europe with the invitations of big countries that were in trouble with their populations and had been suffering from the deficient workers that would work and rebuild those countries after WW2's aftermaths. Turks were not the one nation to go abroad in order to work. South European countries such as Portugal, Spain and Greece also involved in this migration. However, Turks' population was much more than the others. Turkish people mainly migrated to Germany, France, Holland, United Kingdom and Belgium. This number increased day by day and still Turks have been dominating Europe as migrants with their higher populations. Europe is in need of the young population in order to maintain their future and of a new generation that is going to work. However, they do not seem to be fond of Turkish migrants when examined carefully. In the last years, some nationalist groups started to hunt and kill Turkish migrants brutally in Germany[3]. Some less brutal but quite offensive events happened in Denmark, too. In the last weeks, France accepted the Armenian Genocide issue officially and many Turk migrants fury at this decision. Now, they will have to pay an extreme fee in case they deny the Armenian Genocide in the borders of France[4]. These kind of events show us that European societies have not been keen on Turks at all. Nor do they want Turkey as a new brother in Europe family.

According to the researches, the migration of Turks to Europe has been still on. Each year, several Turkish students and married couples migrate to Europe for a better life. In case Turkey becomes an EU member, the migration can get intensified. Refik Erzan, Umut

---

[3] German extremists' murdering Turks: http://www.todayszaman.com/news-262530-german-right-wing-extremists-proud-of-killing-turks.html
[4] France's Armenian Genocide approval: http://www.bbc.co.uk/news/world-europe-16297414

Turkey and EU: What Does the Society Think?

Kuzubaş and Nilüfer Yıldız's work named 'Immigration Scenarios: Turkey–EU' (2006) that was based on the South European countries' experiences such as Portugal, Spain and Greece which had been already EU members.

The studies based on the experiences of the other EU countries indicate a possible migration scenario from Turkey to Europe in case Turkey becomes a full member of European Union. In terms of politics, Turkey is the second largest country in Europe after Germany. If Turkey becomes a member of EU, it is going to have more chairs in EU parliament than the others with its superiority speaking of population. It is not something what Europe would look forward, though.

What Does Turkish Society Think About EU?

After analyzing Europe's side, now it is time to explain the Turks' viewpoints about EU and how they approach to European Union au fond. It is quite obvious that EU does not crave for Turkish membership. However, the situation is the same with Turks. Some Turks do not seem to be eager to be a part of EU for some cultural, religious and historical reasons that give a shape to their minds. More than %99 of the population is Muslim on IDs. However, Turkey does not have any religion politically. Turkey can be a secular country but Islam is the main religion in the borders. European Union is a Christian organization since its member countries' major religion is Christianity. For that reason, most of the Turks who are strong believers do not approve the membership in that they strongly believe that European countries' Christian morals do not fit in Islamic morals of Turkish life style. It does not mean that Turks are narrow-minded and intolerant against the other religions. Unlike, Turks are quite tolerant toward the other religions. It is very clear when searched the minorities' lives living in Turkey. They are not asked about their religions and have the same rights with

Muslim Turks. However, those who support conservatism in terms of politics are worried about the future of Islam and they claim that Islam is going to be underestimated and not respected if we become a member of EU. It is a common fear among the old generation as well as middle-aged people whose beliefs are very strong as well as the prejudices. Religion can be one of the main reasons the historical debates must be also taken into the consideration. Those who oppose to EU membership, also the ones who think that Turkey must be either a part of Arab World or of the Central Asia. They claim that European Union membership is going to make people forget about their roots, from where they came, and what they lived during the WW1 and afterwards. They still tend to hold grudge against the European countries since they have some extreme ideas such as turning out to be military country. There was always a confliction between Turks and the Europeans in terms of culture that was made up of Islam religion as well as Turkish genetics. Turks lived several problems with European countries in the past since they came to Anatolia. Some Turks still believe that this confliction is not going to come to an end and in the end Turks will lose their identities because of the European Union. I have tried to explain the basic opposition reasons of the Turks' who do not want to be a part of EU speaking of my experience that I gained making an online survey on some social networks.

However, the situation for Turkey is not so vague as thought. According to Ali Çarkoğlu's work named 'Turkey and EU: Who wants full membership?' (2003), more than the half of Turkish people including the minorities such as Kurds and Zazas want to be an EU member for several reasons like economics, education, social benefits of being a part of European Union. On the scheme located below, we can see that how many people want to be a part of European Union beside what their roots and political views are. When the scheme analyzed, it can be noticed that Kurdish people's enthusiasm about EU is higher than Turkish people. I would like to explain this situation with the identity crisis of Kurds in the last decades in

Turkey. Kurds believe that European Union can solve the minority problems in a fair way and also they can migrate to Europe and have better life conditions. Today, there are lots of Kurds living abroad, especially in Scandinavian countries, who claimed they were discriminated by Turks. For that reason, they had a chance to go abroad and live there. It is one of the aims of Kurdish people who want full membership whole heartedly.

Turks who are eager for European membership have different reasons from Kurds. They want to improve their lives at the stage of Europeans and want to be accepted by those who have prejudices which I explained in the previous section against Turks. They desire to benefit from the better education conditions of this continent. European Universities are much better than Turkish ones and one of the reasons why Turkish students highly participate in Erasmus Exchange Programme. After going back to Turkey, these students talk about the Western life style in Europe and how good universities are. After Erasmus experience, several students want to have a Master degree in European Universities since they are highly appreciated in Turkey. The people, who live difficulties with Turkish justice system apply for European Court of Human Rights, complain about the current system in Turkey and want it to change over. The people who experience some problems about trade demand a quick and safe system like in Europe. All these people and more require a better life which has more qualified and improved in terms of politics, economics, education and human rights.

Conclusion

In this study, I have explained the EU and Turkey relations from both aspects in terms of the social structures of them. I also mentioned the main reasons why European Union hesitates about Turkey's membership and how Turkish society approaches to EU and expects from it. After all, it seems like European Union does not know what to do with Turkey and for that reason, Turkey has been waited for four decades. They keep Turkey waiting giving hope but not meeting the expectations. Apart from that, new Turkish government has a clear Islamic and conservative line that does not fit in European Union's rough rules. AKP is in a dilemma because it both mentions Arab Brotherhood and wants to participate in Europe. These mutual dilemmas, concerns and unknown reasons behind the visible ones make this relationship tougher. I am of opinion that Turkey needs European Union more than any country does. Besides, Europe cannot dominate Middle East without Turkey and it is obviously in need of a bridge to provide that. Why to play the tricky games instead of cooperating? I do think that both European Union and Turkey have to make up their minds and determine what they expect from each other and how they can meet each others' expectations. Unless given a clear decision about the tense relations among them, Turkey is going to be in limbo. So is European Union. So to maintain the last-longing relationship that has been going on for ages, they both should get rid of the opinionated ideas and prejudices if they look forward to strengthening the relations and make use of that wise cooperation.

References

Diez Thomas, Agnantopoulos Apostolos & Kaliber Alper(2005): File: Turkey,

Europeanization and Civil Society: Introduction,

South European Society and Politics, 10:1, 1-15

Heper Metin (2005): The European Union, the Turkish Military and Democracy,

South European Society and Politics, 10:1, 33-44

Diez Thomas (2005): Turkey, the European Union and Security Complexes Revisited,

Mediterranean Politics, 10:2, 167-180

Erzan Refik, Kuzubaş Umut & Yıldız Nilüfer (2006): Immigration

Scenarios: Turkey–EU,

Turkish Studies, 7:1, 33-44

Tekin Ali, Sharing Sovereignty: Turkey's Sovereignty Culture and the EU Accession

Sovereignty and European Unity

Turin Conference, 12-15 September 2007

Müftüler-Bac Meltem, The never-ending story: Turkey and the European Union

Middle Eastern Studies; Oct 1998; 34, 4; Wilson Social Sciences Abstracts

Erdoğdu Erkan, Turkey and Europe: Undivided but not United

MPRA Paper No. 26928, posted 23. November 2010 / 21:23

M. McLaren Lauren, Explaining Opposition to Turkish Membership of the EU

Turkey and EU: What Does the Society Think?

European Union Politics; DOI: 10.1177/1465116507076432

Volume 8 (2): 251–278

Çarkoğlu Ali (2003): Who Wants Full Membership? Characteristics of Turkish Public Support for EU Membership,

Turkish Studies, 4:1, 171-194